For All the Witches

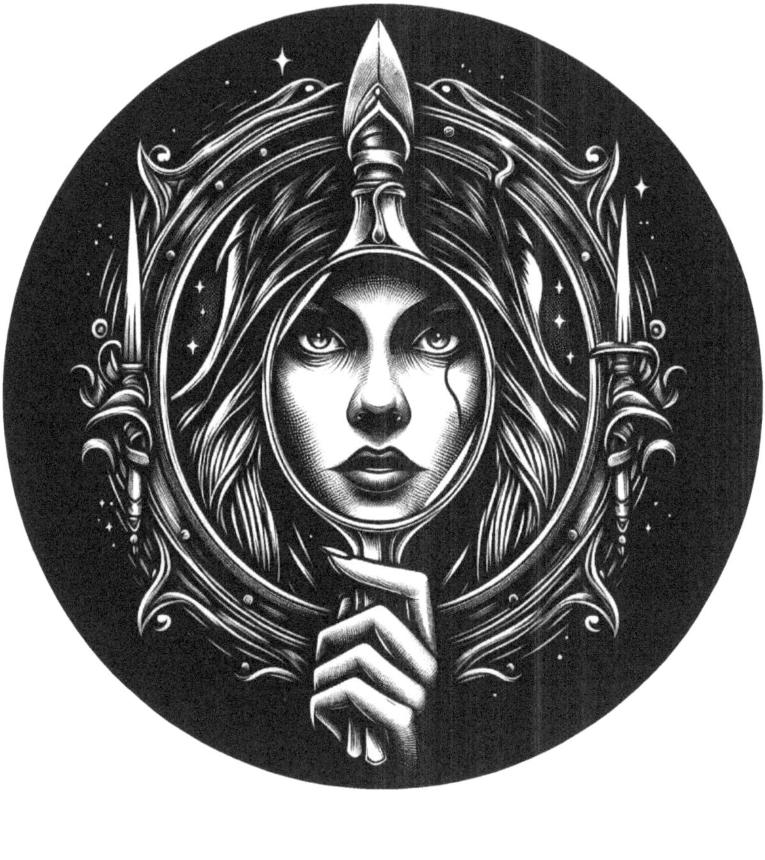

All Nature has both positive and negative aspects and both are necessary to harness the power of Magic. Magic is a manipulation of energy; thoughts, desires and visualisation are forms of energy.

With each spell you must know what you want, see it, feel it and direct it!

Negative dark forces in spells are needed for strength and protection, just as in alchemy, without dark there is no light and without dark we will never comprehend the beauty of the light.

This straight forward book of spells draws on both dark and light, but with an inclusion of a rule Do No Harm unto others.

These spells can be performed at any time of day.

Spells are spontaneous and greater emphasis is on ones desire for a spell -not waiting for the phases of the moon!

Before performing these spells and rituals, make sure you are not disturbed by electronic devices and are in a private room away from distractions.

Do not waste your energy and perform one spell at the time.

All the illustrations have been specifically crafted for this book so you can meditate on them and visualise the spell better!

PROTECTIVE GEMSTONES

Charge and cleanse your crystals before and after use under sun or moonlight, or in salt for 1 day.

Hematite: Protection /Grounding to Earth.

Onyx: Black onyx absorbs negative energy giving wearer power and emotional strength.

Jet: Filters negative energies and outside negative influences in your daily life.

Obsidian: A powerful gemstone with strong psychic protection, shielding you against all negative influences.

Labradorite: Protection against psychic attacks and energy vampires.

Black Tourmaline: A rare and powerful gemstone.

Shungite: Is a very powerful mineral stone almost 2 billion years old. Use it for purifying and grounding.

Amber is another stone which is good for grounding and balancing emotions.

Make sure all of these gemstones are black in colour, as black repels negativity better! Place the stones around your home or wear them as jewellery.

LOVE GEMSTONES

Rose Quartz: The most powerful of love gemstone. Attracting love and improving self love. Pink colour works best!

Carnelian: To bring passion into your life.

Pink Morganite: To bring affection & love.

Kunzite: A rare gemstone for divine love associated with the heart energy.

Lepidolite: A transforming healing stone that helps to dissolve past traumas and promote calm. **Amethyst** stone is also used for same purposes.

Pink Tourmaline: Soothing stone for self love, anxiety, open heart and unconditional love.

Larimar: Soulmate stone, brings hope and tranquillity, and promotes lasting love.

,

PURIFYING RITUAL BATH

You can prepare this bath before performing any of the rituals and spells, or to remove negativity and curses.

Prepare bath water and add muslin bag containing herbs:

Lavender
Marjoram
Calendula (Dried Marigold Flowers)
Rosemary
Burdock Root

Add the muslin bag with herbs and sprinkle coarse sea salt into the tub. Mix the water clockwise 3 times with your hand.

If herbs are not available you can also use a drop of apple vinegar to your bath. Vinegar removes, cleans and repels. Once in the bath, gather handfuls of vinegar water and pour the water over your head.
Soak in the bath and feel all negativity evaporate.

FREEZE OUT A PERSON

This is a spell to banish a person from contacting you and freezing them out from your thoughts. It works especially well after a breakup when you want to disconnect from them energetically and stop having thoughts about them.

Get a plain piece of paper and with a black pen write the full name of the person.
Fold the paper 3 times outwards and place the paper in the freezer.
Keep it in the freezer until you feel better and you have iced them out of your life!

EGG SPELL TO REMOVE CURSE

Eggs are considered one of the most ancient symbols of mankind. This egg spell will absorb negative energy and any curses placed on you.

Get 1 raw white egg
1 makeshift tray made out of a piece of foil
(Tear a small piece of foil and make a small tray where one egg will fit into snugly).

Place the egg inside the foil tray and place it under your bed for 3 days. Do not touch the egg!
After 3 days have passed remove the egg from your bed with the foil tray.
Break the egg and pour it down the toilet. Envision the curse breaking. Flush it!

POPPY SEED SPELL

In ancient times poppy flower heads were worn to attract luck and abundance. In cooking the seeds are used to induce love.

If you feel your beloved one is losing interest; sprinkle a few poppy seeds inside their shoes.
This will prevent them from straying and being unfaithful!

GODDESS LOVE OIL

Make sure the essential oils below are suitable for skin contact. You will need :

1 glass jar 500 ml with a lid
35 or 50 ml glass pipette bottle

Grapeseed or Almond essential oil as a carrier oil
25 drops Bergamot
49 drops Rose oil
2 tsp Orris Root or Myrrh oil
15 drops Lavender oil
Do not create this oil if you are allergic to any of the ingredients listed.

Add the following in same order to the glass jar:

Myrrh or Orris Root & Rose oil

Top the jar with **Grapeseed or Almond oil** and seal.

Allow the oil to infuse for 1 week, gently shaking the jar everyday. After 1 week add **Lavender & Bergamot oil.**

Shake the jar and add the oil into glass pipette. Shake the oil and use it for body massage, bath or anointing candle rituals to draw love in.

DO NOT LET PEOPLE AFFECT YOU

This is a simple spell to stop people's opinions and ill will affect your psyche. It will put a block on their energy.

Write down the person's full name on a small piece of paper once in black ink.
With melted wax from a Black candle, seal and cover their name completely with hot wax.
Fold the paper the paper outwards 3 times.
Bury the paper in soil.

SEX MAGIC

This spell harnesses the divine power of sexual energy to manifest. Before just coming to an orgasm with your partner, make you intent known to yourself and the universe. Visualise it. Focus your energy on what you want to manifest in your life and believe in it.

EGG LOVE SPELL

For this spell, you will need 1 raw white egg and a small piece of paper.
On a small piece of paper write down the full name of the intended in red pen.
Roll the paper into a tiny scroll.

With a small needle or a similar tool, open a small hole on top of the egg.
Push down the scroll inside the egg hole and put it in the freezer.
As long as the name is in the egg and the egg is intact, the intended will only think of you!
When you feel the spell has worked, bury the intact egg in soil.

GUIDE TO MOON PHASES

You can follow the phases of the moon to conduct your spells and rituals if you wish.

New Moon: Start new projects, for new love & new beginnings.
Waxing Crescent: To manifest your desires into your life.
Waxing Gibbous: For money & prosperity.
Full Moon: For manifestations, psychic energy, banishment and cleansing.
Waning Gibbous: To expel all negativity.
Waning Quarter: For cleaning, de-cluttering your home and removing unwanted things in your life.
Waning Crescent: To cleanse your space and aura.

BLESSED HOUSE JARS

You will need 4 clear glass jars with a lid whichever sized you prefer.

In Jar 1 fill it up with coarse sea salt . This will be for Protection.

In Jar 2 put dried Lavender flowers. This will be for peace and harmony.

In Jar 3 put dried rose petals. This will be for love.

In Jar 4 put raw White Rice. This will be for wealth.

Fill the jars to the top and scatter them around your home. The 4 jars will symbolise North, East, South and West of your house.

TO WARD OF EVIL AND BAD LUCK

Red Chilli peppers have been know for centuries to protect against evil eye, jealousy and dispel bad luck. The heat of the peppers will dispel gossip and ill will.

Hang a garland of dried red chilli peppers near the main entrance of your home or above the door. This will create a "shield of fire" from bad energy.

LOVE HERBS & ESSENTIAL OILS

Clary
Jasmine
Neroli
Patchouli
Rose
Sandalwood
Ylang-Ylang
Orris Root
Basil Yarrow
Cinnamon
Vanilla
Coriander

LOVE HERBS

Cardamom: For love & passion.
Add cardamom, rose petals and cinnamon stick to a small muslin bag and carry it as an attraction charm.
Vanilla Bean: For love & lust.
Cinnamon: Helps to create passion between lovers.
Thyme: For loyalty and affection.
Rosemary: For love & fidelity. Helps for long a lasting relationship and unity.
Basil: Loving vibrations. Bathe in basil to attract new romance.
Saffron: Used in magic for love.
Caraway Seeds & Poppy seeds: Used in keeping a loved one faithful. Make some food for your beloved containing these seeds.
Marjoram: Strengthens love & relationships.
Orris Root: An ancient magical herb for love. Combine with Jasmine to draw in love.
Patchouli: For passion, sensuality and magnetism.
Pink Rose: Love & affection.
Dark Red Rose: Passionate intense love.
Vanilla: For sexiness, attraction & irresistibility. Powerful when combined with rose in a perfume.
Damiana: For love, sex and magic.
For simple rituals you can utilise them in cooking, find them in the ingredients list of a perfume or make your own love oil!

MAGICAL PHRASE FOR LUCK

This phrase will radically change your mood for the better and attract luck. Repeat this phrase 30 times a day.

" ALL MY TROUBLES DISAPPEAR ONLY GOOD LUCK WILL APPEAR."

HERBS & ESSENTIAL OILS FOR ANXIETY

Bergamot
Lavender
Mandarin
Grapefruit
Vervain
Witch Hazel
Chamomile
Sage
Frankincense
Geranium
Juniper
Gotu Kala

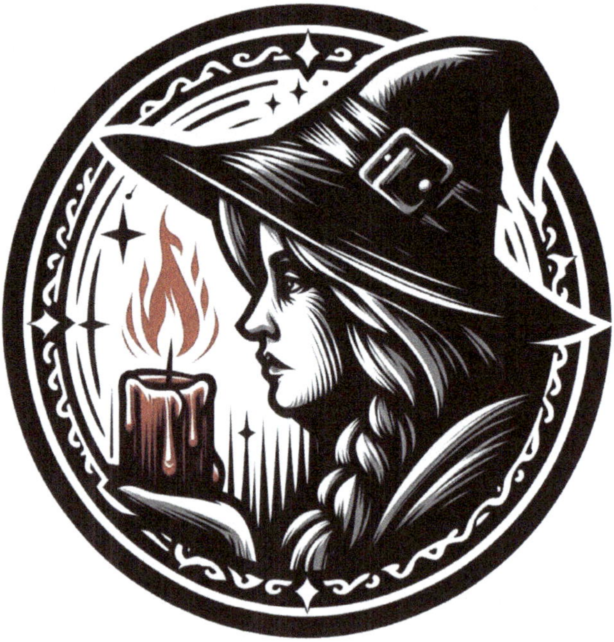

CANDLE LOVE SPELL

1 Red Candle
1 needle or inscribing tool
1 piece of white paper
Red pen

On white piece of paper write down the full name of your intended and what you want in red pen.

Fold the paper 3 times towards yourself.

Inscribe the full name of your crush on the red candle with a needle.

Anoint the candle with a love oil of your choice, rubbing the candle downwards.

Place the folded paper under the candle.

Light the candle. Stare into the flame and focus on your desires for 3 minutes. Let the candle burn down.

Carry the paper on you until your goal has been achieved.

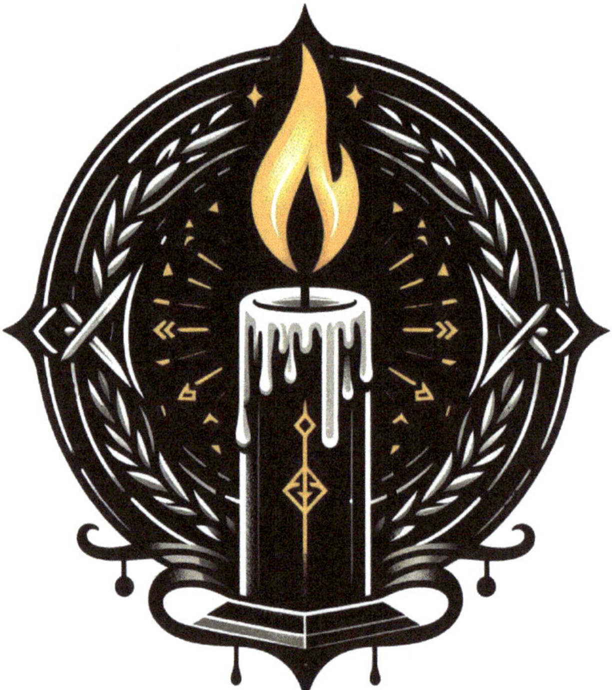

CANDLE PUNISHMENT SPELL

This spell is a punishment towards a person who has wronged you. This spell is not to wish ill will, but to provide a lesson for the intended.

> 1 Needle or inscribing tool
> White piece of paper
> Black Candle
> Black pen

Inscribe the persons name (if the full name just write the first name) on the black candle who has wronged you or cursed you.
On a piece of white paper, write down all what the person did to you, their full name and why you want them to be punished. This spell is not for harm, but to teach them a lesson no to repeat similar deeds. Fold the paper away from you 3 times.Place the paper under the black candle, light the candle and stare into the flame feeling the punishment being returned to the intended and all the wrong they did to you. The candle flame should soothe your anger and injustice.Let the candle burn down completely and throw away the folded piece of paper.

CANDLE MONEY SPELL

1 Green Candle
1 piece of white paper
Green pen
Couple of bay leaves
Peppermint oil

On white piece of paper write down your intentions with a green pen. A new job, success, extra money etc. Fold the paper 3 times towards yourself.
Anoint the candle with peppermint oil, rubbing the candle downwards. Place bay leaves around the candle and folded paper under the candle. Light the candle. Stare into the flame and focus on your desires for 3 minutes. Do this until the candle burns down. Carry the paper inside your wallet until your goal is achieved.

BANISH EVIL SPIRITS

Take a hand bell that is loud enough.
Walk around the room you feel the presence of evil spirits. Walk towards each corner of the room and ring the bell into each corner 3 times.

Reciting:
" I am cleansing every corner of the room."

After, light a white or yellow unscented candle.
And walk again to each corner of the room with the candle, purifying the space with candle flame.
Leave a couple of large white mints in the room for peace.

After this ritual take a shower with sea salt for protection and purification.

CUT PSYCHIC CORDS

This spell will help with heartbreak, toxic emotional ties and obsession.

Black Pen
A4 Paper
Red marker
Scissors

On an A4 paper draw 2 stick figures opposite each with space in between them. One figure will represent you and the other will be the person you want to cut the connection with.
With a red marker draw lines connecting the stick figures. Starting from top of the head, 3rd eye, throat, heart, stomach, genitals and feet.

Example:

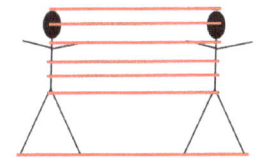

The 7 red cords symbolize the cords that bind you and your 7 energy centres.
Cut the red lines with scissors one by one slowly though the middle, separating the figures. Visualise the emotional tie being cut. After, rip the paper and throw the papers away.

REVERSE THE CURSE

Mirrors are used for divination, harnessing the power of the moon & sun, and for looking into the future. This mirror spell is for reversing the curse back unto the person who cast it on you.

Buy a new mirror, any size will do! Wash the mirror in salt water to prepare it for the spell. You will use this mirror only once for this spell.

With a black marker pen, write your full name on the mirror 3 times. Think about how you have been cursed, the injustice which befell upon you and what you want them to stop doing. If you know the person who has cursed you, imagine the reflection of your name coming back to them as silver lightning bolts.

And recite 3 times:

"Whatever you wished upon me, let it come back to you thrice!"

After, throw it away. Do no reuse this mirror.

TO MAKE YOUR LOVER MISS YOU

Take 2 matchsticks with a red or pink tips.
One matchstick will be you and the other one your beloved.
Light a small red candle. Focus on the flame and think about the outcome you desire.
Name the matchsticks out loud with your name and your beloved.

Light both matchsticks from the red candle flame until both are lit.
Holding them together in one hand, let them burn till near the end and recite:

*" As the matches burn ,
Let his heart burn for me with love and longing."*

Let the red candle burn down till the end.

FAST ENERGY CLEANSING SPELL

This spell is to quickly get rid of bad omens and bad mood. Pour sea salt with a spoon into your left hand and close the hand. Meditate, absorbing the salt in your hand.

Recite:

" Salt cleanse me, take all the bad energy from me !"

Meditate for 3 minutes and wash your hand in water.

PROTECTION JAR

You will need a clear glass jar with a lid, wide enough to fit crystals in.

Put inside the jar:
Red Dried Chilli pepper, Sea Salt crystals, Black Tourmaline, Sage, Jet crystal, Obsidian crystal, Onyx.

Seal the jar with a lid and place the jar in a visible place of your home or the room you feel uneasy in. Keep the jar until you feel protected. After, bury the jar in soil. Do not reuse the jar.

LOVE JAR

You will need a clear glass jar which is wide enough to fit crystals in.
Put the following inside the jar: a couple of Sugar Cubes, Dried Rose Petals, Pink Salt, Orris Root, Cinnamon stick, Pink Rose quartz or any other love crystal.

On a piece of paper write down in red pen your intentions for love.
Make the paper into a scroll and put it inside a jar.
Seal the jar with a lid and place the jar in a visible place of your home.
Keep the jar until you see results in love.
After, bury the jar in soil. Do not reuse the jar.

MONEY JAR

You will need a clear glass jar with a lid which is wide enough to fit crystals in,
Put the following crystals inside the jar: Pyrite, Malachite, Aventurine, Citrine.
Put Dried Herbs inside the jar: Alfalfa, Patchouli, Bay Leaf, Rosemary.

On a piece of paper write down in green pen your intentions for money.
Make the paper into a scroll and put it inside a jar.
Seal the jar with a lid and place the jar in a visible place of your home. Keep the jar until you see results in money. After, bury the jar in soil. Do not reuse the jar.

Citrine is a versatile gemstone known also as the Merchant Stone which is associated with wealth and success.
Place a small Citrine crystal inside your wallet to draw in luck !

Aventurine is another special crystal with with its green hues which can aide you with success and luck! Carry it on you when you need a second chance in finances or for an important business meeting!

Orris Root

Pomme D'Amour

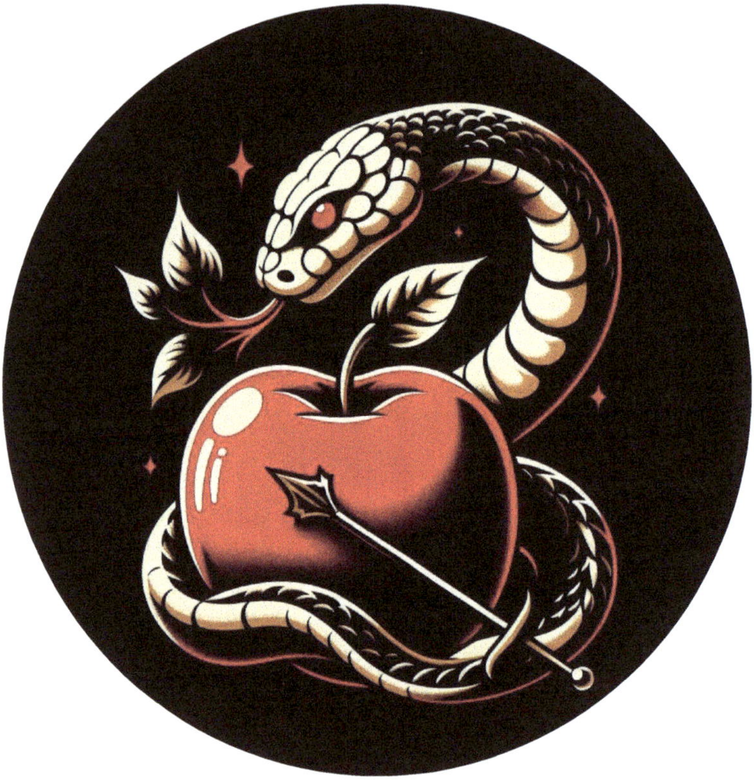

RETAIN YOUR POWER

1. Talk Less

2. Be calm

3. Observe more

4. Make eye contact

5. Think before you speak

6. Manage your time

7. Be respectful to ALL

8. Move in silence

Intro, 2-3

Protective Gemstones, 4-5

Love Gemstones, 6-7

Purifying Ritual Bath, 8-9

Freeze Out Spell, 10-11

Egg Spell for Curse, 12-13

Poppy Seed Spell, 14-15

Goddess Love, 16-17

Do no Let People Affect You, 18-19

Egg Love Spell, 20-21

Blessed Home Jar, 22-23

Love Herbs & Essential Oils, 24-25

For Luck, 26

Herbs & Essential Oils for Anxiety, 27

Candle Love Spell, 28-29

Candle Punishment Spell, 30-31

Candle Money Spell, 32

Banish Evil Spirits, 33

Cut Psychic Cord, 34-35

Reverse the Curse, 36-37

Make Lover Miss You, 38-39

Energy Cleansing Spell, 40

Protection Jar, 41

Love Jar, 42

Money Jar, 43

Money Crystals, 44-45

Retain You Power, 48-49

Milton Keynes UK
Ingram Content Group UK Ltd.
UKHW021141100324
439183UK00002B/27